Huakaʻi Hele
LONG VOYAGE

THE HALIʻA ALOHA SERIES

Huaka'i Hele
LONG VOYAGE

SALLY-JO KEALA-O-ĀNUENUE BOWMAN

THE HALI'A ALOHA SERIES
Darien Hsu Gee, Series Editor

Hali'a Aloha ("Cherished memories") by Legacy Isle Publishing is a guided memoir program developed in collaboration with series editor Darien Hsu Gee. The series celebrates moments big and small, harnessing the power of short forms to preserve the lived experiences of the storytellers. To become a Hali'a Aloha author, please visit www.legacyislepublishing.net.

Legacy Isle Publishing is an imprint of Watermark Publishing, based in Honolulu, Hawai'i, and dedicated to "Telling Hawai'i's Stories" through memoirs, corporate biographies, family histories and other books.

© 2020 Sally-Jo Keala-o-Ānuenue Bowman

All rights reserved. No part of this book may be reproduced in any form or by any electronic or mechanical means, including information retrieval systems, without prior written permission from the publisher, except for brief passages quoted in reviews.

ISBN 978-1-948011-45-7 (print)
ISBN 978-1-948011-46-4 (e-book)

Design and production
Dawn Sakamoto Paiva

Legacy Isle Publishing
1000 Bishop St., Ste. 806
Honolulu, HI 96813
Telephone 1-808-587-7766
Toll-free 1-866-900-BOOK
www.legacyislepublishing.net

Printed in the United States

He hoʻomanaʻo
In memory of
Anuhea Nahale-ā

Also by Sally-Jo Keala-o-Ānuenue Bowman

The Heart of Being Hawaiian
No Footprints in the Sand: A Memoir of Kalaupapa
with Henry Nalaielua

CONTENTS

Princess Kaʻiulani and the Old Gray Mare 1
Huakaʻi 7
Sales Career 15
Father of Waters 17
O Noble Toothbrush 28
The Way Back 29
Embers 33
Back to the Bastion 36
Teacups and Dolls 50
Aloha, Ojibwa 52
Mother's Night 58
Gifts from the Sea 63
Voice of the Beloved 64
A Closing Conversation 1987 69
Thank You, J.P. Sousa 75
Being Hawaiian 78
Dozens of Cousins 84
Aloha, Anuhea 87
No Na Pua 92
True Gratitude 97
Acknowledgments 100
Publication Notes 102

PRINCESS KAʻIULANI AND THE OLD GRAY MARE
2004

The email said: "I asked all my cousins who had lived at Kaʻiulani Home if they remembered the song about Kaʻiulani. They all said no, they don't think the song even exists. I think you and Jackie are both having big, fat brain farts."

The message was from my classmate Nanette—"Titi" to intimates, which is to say, everybody except the IRS. She, Jackie, myself and maybe a dozen of our slightly older or younger sisters and cousins had spent our first boarding year at Kamehameha Schools in the early 1950s at Kaʻiulani Home in downtown Honolulu. It was a desperate measure on the part of the Girls School, which had too many boarders to house on the Kapālama Heights campus.

A couple of weeks before the email, Titi, Jackie and I had celebrated the golden anniversary of our friendship. To mark it, we visited the site of Kaʻiulani Home at 567 South King Street and tried to sing songs we'd learned when we were twelve.

The old board-and-batten house named for the tragic princess who died in 1899 had long since been replaced with the concrete and glass of Kawaiahaʻo Plaza.

When we lived there in 1952 to 1953, an enormous full-length oil portrait of the beautiful Kaʻiulani loomed over us in the parlor. Rubber-treaded steps formed a central interior staircase that split left and right, leading to two wings of a dozen or so rooms. Each was spartanly equipped with a set of bunk beds, two desks, two chairs and two dressers, the surface of which we each were expected to cover with one of the two dresser scarves from the precise list of items we were to bring with us.

Outside, the yard was bounded in front by a waist-high, wrought iron, picket fence and a hedge running along King Street. Behind a high wooden fence in the back was the Mission Homes complex.

Every day, forty of us little girls commuted by private school bus to the campus. I mean every day, weekends included. On Sundays, we attended church in the school auditorium, stiff as soldiers in the starched white dresses required for the Sabbath and other special occasions. Saturday evenings, the school bus also transported us upward for the weekly supervised social event with students from the Boys School. Often it was a movie; sometimes it was a "play night" featuring various outdoor games.

Our housemothers, Mrs. Chang and Mrs. Vincent, regimented our hours at Kaʻiulani Home. Mrs. Chang was a tiny Chinese-Hawaiian grandmother in sling-back high heels. She dyed her hair black and swept it up to gain some height, the better to be supremely effective when she bored her black eyes right through a little girl's spine. Mrs. Vincent was her assistant, hardly any bigger, an ancient paper-skinned *haole* with violet-blue eyes and white hair done flawlessly in the same stylish upsweep. Many of the girls took to Mrs. Vincent, but some of them hummed "The Old Gray Mare" behind her back. Mrs. V's white hair was the inspiration, but Mrs. Chang shared equally in the dedication of the song.

It may have been our housemothers' joint hope that the after-school schedule for us—scrubbing our laundry with our knuckles against tin washboards, raking the curling red *kamani* leaves that fell daily from the tree in the side yard, polishing the dark and dreary *koa* furniture beneath the princess's portrait—would keep all forty little girls too busy, as they say, to make humbug.

It worked for us wimps. But Jackie was much tougher.

We had not been at Kaʻiulani Home more than a couple of weeks when Jackie climbed out her second-story window into the limbs of the kamani tree. About the moment she settled herself in the branches, Mrs. Chang happened to stroll out of her office near the front door onto the walkway that circled the house. And she looked up.

"Jac - que - line! You get inside!"

The rules didn't specify "no climbing out windows" or "no perching in trees," but there seemed to be one big blanket unspoken rule that prohibited everything a twelve-year-old tomboy might naturally do. The 687 specific rules that outlined what we were expected to do struck us as ridiculous: Make your bed with hospital corners. Bedspread must have no wrinkles. Always break your piece of bread in quarters before buttering it. Wash your hairbrush and comb every Thursday and check them in with the Old Gray Mare on duty. Certainly you were not to leave the grounds.

All this goes to say that at Ka'iulani Home, Jackie was doomed.

One afternoon, her after-school job was to squirt dirt and leaves off King Street's public sidewalk, which was outside the iron fence. While she wielded the hose and nozzle, teenage boys cruised by in a convertible, cat-calling and wolf-whistling at Jackie in her shorts. She hollered back.

Still, she might have escaped the notice of Mrs. Chang, except the boys decided that getting a rise out of Jackie was worth repeating. When they came slowly along King Street again, Jackie was ready. They hooted at her, and she doused them all—just as Mrs. Chang came out the front door.

"Jac - que - line!"

On Saturdays, most of us—Titi and I included—put on one of our two perfectly starched and ironed "outing dresses" and went to the matinee movies downtown at the Princess or Hawaii theaters. Jackie always had so many hours of detention to serve on Saturdays that she didn't get out of Ka'iulani Home until Thanksgiving vacation.

One Saturday, Mrs. Chang assigned her and another sinner to scrub the concrete floor of the wash house. Jackie the tree climber was not only athletic, but also creative. Before long, she and her partner had a game of hockey going, with scrub brooms for sticks and a cake of soap for the puck. Inevitably, Jackie hit the puck, sending it sailing soapily out the door onto the walkway, just as Mrs. Vincent came to check on the girls' progress.

The episode may have been a first—getting detention while serving detention.

Fifty years later, surviving the whole year at Ka'iulani Home seemed like something to celebrate.

The three of us bought *lei* and took them to 567 S. King Street. Although no trace of the old house remained, the iron fence was still there. A park bench and a public restroom occupied the spot where the wash house had stood. In the 'Ewa side yard, the old kamani tree shaded coarse grass. Someone had encased the base in a concrete planter in which a thicket of *laua'e* ferns grew.

We leaned our *'okole* against the rim of the planter, looking at our shadowy images in the glass walls of the new building as if they were rotund gray ghosts of little girls.

After we left our lei for Princess Ka'iulani in the tree, Jackie said, "OK, we have to sing."

"What?"

"The song to Ka'iulani."

But none of us could remember it. Titi didn't think it had ever existed.

"OK, we'll sing something else," Jackie said, and then launched right into:

*"The old gray mare
She ain't what she used to be!"*

The song seemed as pertinent as it had been fifty years before. We all laughed. And on the next downbeat, Titi and I joined in, belting out the rest of the words under the old kamani tree:

*"Ain't what she used to be,
Ain't what she used to be.
The old gray mare
She ain't what she used to be,
Many long years ago."*

HUAKAʻI
2008

Huakaʻi. It means "journey." When I started on the journey that became the book *The Heart of Being Hawaiian*, I had yet to learn the word huakaʻi. It was 1984.

Twenty years later, when I was nearing the end of the quest for my Hawaiian roots I met Kapono Souza, a young Hawaiian man who had decided in 2001 to model his own *huakaʻi* on an ancient practice during the four-month Hawaiian winter. During those Makahiki months of peace and rest, an entourage of chiefs and priests circled their island on foot, stopping at villages for games, entertainments and feasts, and to collect annual tribute from the people. Wanting to understand the ancient rite, Kapono began what became his annual walk around Oʻahu. Lacking a retinue, he did his huakaʻi alone.

"At night," he said, "everything smells different, the *maile lau liʻi*, the sea, the rain. I hear the ocean, the wind, the mongoose in the bush. These are the sounds the ancestors heard. They smelled the *maile*, the *pili* grass in Nānākuli. Night is the time when you can pick up on *hōʻailona*, signs, interpreting them in ways that make sense. It's a time of insight." What I learned from Kapono I wrote in "The Long Walk Home" for *Hana Hou!* magazine.

This piece of my own solo journey appeared first as the introduction to *The Heart of Being Hawaiian* (Watermark Publishing, 2008), a collection of previously published articles and essays about parts of modern Hawaiian culture. Only years after the last of these pieces had appeared, in nine magazines and three anthologies, was I able to see that they should be arranged not in order of when I wrote them, but in themes that revealed layers of the Hawaiian heart.

The figurative and indeliberate route of my huakaʻi twisted and turned as it went along, like the Old Pali Road I traversed many times as a Kailua kid on the grand, infrequent adventure of "going to town." At first, all I knew for sure was my desire to write about a culture I felt I didn't know well enough, even though I was quarter Hawaiian and a graduate of Kamehameha Schools.

In the beginning, not only did I not know the meaning of "huakaʻi," I did not even set off on a quest. My intention was to become a full-time freelance magazine writer. But I unconsciously put myself on this particular path in 1984 when I finished a Journalism Master's Degree at the University of Oregon with a lengthy final writing project called "On the Winds of Kanaloa: Rebirth of the Hawaiian People."

At that time I had already lived on the mainland U.S. for twenty-six years, first at the University of Minnesota following my 1958 graduation from Kamehameha Schools, and then in Oregon. I did come back to Hawai'i every summer during college to work as a cub reporter for the *Honolulu Star-Bulletin*, and then every couple of years to visit my parents for a week or two. It wasn't enough, but I didn't know that then.

When I did the "Winds of Kanaloa" field research in Hawai'i, my first interview was with Adelaide "Frenchy" DeSoto, who had recently badgered the state legislature into creating the Office of Hawaiian Affairs. She had much to say on the subject of the so-called Hawaiian Renaissance, but what affected me most was her huge hug. Had the *honi* been relearned then, she might have stunned me with the nose-to-nose greeting, which, at that time, I had never experienced. Her hug had a similar effect. Having lived away so long, I felt like a foreigner, and I didn't expect such warmth from a woman I had never met. Her *aloha* filled the air. I felt so accepted and loved that my eyes filled with tears.

I'd been a journalist since high school days, always in the employ of some corporate or educational entity. When I finished my long master's tome, my goal was full-time freelance writing. For several years, I fit freelancing around working at a regular job, hustling assignments from local and regional magazines in Oregon, going out on the full-time freelance limb in 1991. When I was home in Hawai'i for a visit in late 1988, I attended a concert by the Makaha Sons, a benefit for some preschool. The school turned out to be Pūnana Leo, the then-new Hawaiian-language immersion preschool. In 1988 I'd never heard of Pūnana Leo—but I recognized it as a story idea, which I suggested to *Aloha* magazine. I got the assignment, my first on a Hawaiian topic.

The whole time I'd been away from Hawai'i, "aboriginal twinges" called to me. I had grown up in Kailua, O'ahu, very near the beach. When I went away, I often dreamed of being in the ocean.

I was a kid in the '40s and '50s, a time when it still was not cool to be Hawaiian. My half-Hawaiian father and his siblings were born in the first decade of the twentieth century, the first generation not born in the Kingdom or its predecessors, the several island chiefdoms. They were Americans of the Territory of Hawaii, created in 1900. Under what must have been an uncertain and unsettling political and social climate, at least to adults, their family and lots of others left the Hawaiian language behind, along with many customs and much knowledge.

Kamehameha, my school from seventh through twelfth grade, even though instituted for Hawaiian children, sought to make us thoroughly American. Which I was. Except for those twinges and a gaping hole in my heart.

After the Pūnana Leo story, I consciously—and self-consciously, because I wasn't sure about how I would be received, despite Frenchy DeSoto— pursued article assignments to learn about being

Hawaiian as well as to write about specific topics. I learned about *hula, heiau,* the Hawaiian diet. I spent three days on Kahoʻolawe during January *Makahiki* ceremonies, addressed a personal health problem through *lomilomi,* sailed for an afternoon on the voyaging canoe *Hōkūleʻa*. Eventually I came to know dozens of people in the Hawaiian community. They all welcomed me, especially after I learned to approach any Hawaiian by placing myself in my family, school and community. I think it is today's version of what some have told me was the ancient recitation of genealogy between strangers until they came to a point of commonality. Never mind the journalism degrees and writing achievements. I am the younger Pierre Bowman's older sister, Uncle Wright's niece, Scotty's cousin. I am KS '58. I am Kailua, Oʻahu. Now we can talk.

In a few years, with dozens more Hawaiian articles in print, a significant vestige of the heart *puka* nevertheless remained. Then, in Hilo in late 1997, I met Aunty Abbie Napeahi and Uncle Howard Peʻa. For yet another article, I wanted to learn about the Hawaiian conflict resolution process called *hoʻoponopono*. They were practitioners through the Hawaiian social services agency Alu Like. They answered my questions. But they also saw right into the puka in my heart. How they gave me their down-to-earth blessing is detailed in the essay "Aloha, Anuhea."

For years before I decided to freelance, my professional training in journalism had me keeping my views and orientation out of reporting. But the magazine world is somewhat different, and the Hawaiian world is the opposite. The more projects I took on, the sharper my personal Hawaiian senses became. One of my best editors told me he never wanted to see a piece that didn't have me in it. Someone else told me I was always in my articles even if I never used the word "I." Eventually I wrote occasional essays that weren't based on research but instead were totally about my own experience. Several of these various pieces won Paʻi awards from the Hawaiʻi Publishers' Association. But my most treasured praise was five words from Noa Emmett Aluli, the Molokaʻi doctor who is perhaps the best known Hawaiian activist and with whom I worked on some major assignments. I bumped into Emmett some months after the magazine publication of "Kahoʻolawe in Limbo." He hugged me—there it was again! Aloha hug! And he said, "The Kahoʻolawe piece was great. *Your writing is so Hawaiian.*"

His compliment meant more to me than money, awards or any other accolades. *So Hawaiian.* Those words signaled the beginning of a confidence and gratitude that I was at last finding the Hawaiian: both Hawaiian culture, history and values *and* myself as a Hawaiian.

That was in 1993. Soon, I hit a stride. In 2002 I wrote "Inescapably Hawaiian," the piece I selected to close *The Heart of Being Hawaiian*. In retrospect, it represents *huliau*—another word I learned along the way, which means "turning point" or "time of change." I wrote only two more Hawaiian culture articles after that. The last was the profile of Kapono Souza, "The Long Walk Home."

In the months following its publication in 2004, I felt in my *naʻau*—my heart and guts—that I was done writing Hawaiian articles, even though I certainly had not written on every possible topic. But it wasn't until I was arranging the best of my magazine pieces to make the most sense as a book that I saw that I had been working piecemeal on a quilt, and had come to a point where I could see the whole thing.

I am the keeper of a frail antique Hawaiian quilt. My Hawaiian grandmother, Mele ʻElemakule Pā Bowman, made it around the turn of the twentieth century, when the Hawaiian Kingdom had been overthrown and Hawaiʻi was being annexed by the United States. Her fragile, hand-stitched quilt lay folded in a suitably antique trunk, where I could see only a small part of it. The red cotton design portraying leaves of the *ʻulu*—breadfruit—has faded, and its white background has yellowed with a century of age. The old cotton batting shows through small puka where the fabric has simply disintegrated.

The quilt is too delicate to keep out. And yet, one day a year or so after I wrote about Kapono Souza and his huakaʻi, I laid that quilt upon my bed where I could see the whole thing. That night I slept under it.

Just recently I have seen that I had been stitching a figurative quilt folded over my lap, words substituting for bits of fabric, my pen working as the needle. With that last story, I metaphorically laid the quilt of words upon my bed and saw my work as a whole.

In some places this quilt remains unfinished, but it is complete enough.

The magazine articles and essays are *pau* because I am at that huliau, a time of change. But with every end comes a new beginning. The pieces here are the gift of the huakaʻi, for me, and for you. They are roots, and with the care of a calm and grateful heart, flowers and fruit are sure to follow.

SALES CAREER
2007

I remember writing on my order
"form," penciling in Palmer script
"One box No. 4 assortment, $1.25
Customer: Aunty Nina"

Aunty Margaret ordered fancy,
a box of twenty-five Christmas cards
and some imprinted stationery
with blue scalloped edges
for my cousin Ann
I myself could afford no such thing
because of saving the profits

Those sweat-hot Augusts
before sixth and seventh grade
I made my entrepreneurial
rounds of ten more aunts,
the ladies of our neighborhood
and my mother's other friends
Two or three of the unrelated

resisted my foldout
samples ordered from an ad
in Mama's *Ladies' Home Journal*

But every aunt graciously
chose at least one box
from the catalog of ugly cards
keeping an eye on birthdays to come
maybe even mine
and Christmas too
Only decades later did I realize
that the other eye
was on a little girl already
someday going to college
via the Cheerful Card Company
White Plains NY
twenty-five cents a box

FATHER OF WATERS
1998

At dawn on a Sunday, I swam in a surfless sea. I had swum in these Kailua waters since before I could walk. We lived four house lots beyond the high tide mark. When I was growing up, the beach, with its warm coral sand and sparkling, frothy waves, was just a fact of life.

On this particular morning, I recalled all the years of seaside living, and realized that the ocean was not a scrap of exotic geography to me, but the context for life itself. I had just strewn my brother's ashes in these quiet morning waters, and I lingered in a peace I had never before defined.

When we were little, my mother took us to the beach every morning, and some afternoons. We splashed at low tide, and once I filled Baby Pierre's swim trunks with wet sand as he sat digging. When he got up, his drawers dropped around his ankles like a sand bomb. My mother thwunked me on my fanny when her darling Pierre began to cry, and the wet sand from her hand stung me. But seeing Pierre lose his pants was so funny, it was worth a spank.

...

One morning, instead of walking to the beach, my mother took us past two houses to the main road to watch President Roosevelt ride by in a jeep. She tugged on me as the convoy approached.

"Wave!" she said, and tugged again. "Wave! He's President Roosevelt!" She put her hand over her heart.

This was Hawai'i, 1944. Roosevelt was reviewing the troops at the Naval Air Station not five miles from our home. Three years earlier, the first Japanese bombs had hit the air base, dropped from planes on their way over the mountains to Pearl Harbor. At the time, I didn't know this, but if I had I wouldn't have cared.

I jerked my arm up and flapped my fingers twice. The president waved back, right at me. Then he was gone.

I coughed in the jeep fumes and said, "So can we go to the beach now?"

Usually, as the tide came in and the waves grew, some grown-ups went in the water to body surf. My daddy was good at it, and when the waves weren't too big, he would take me with him.

"Now, don't take her way out," my mother scolded. "She's too little." My mother was from North Dakota. She didn't go way out herself.

"Yeah, yeah," my daddy winked. And he took me beyond the breakers, lifting me under my arms so I could jump the waves with him. Sometimes my mother would signal, motioning us to come back to shore.

"She wants us to go in," I said.

"Yeah, yeah."

He taught me how to watch a swell, to tell by its exact shape whether it would be good to catch. If it was no good and not breaking yet, we jumped it, floating easily upward.

If the wave was starting to break, we'd drive through it head-to-sea, so that the force of the white curl would not smack us. If the wave looked good, my daddy held me just below the ribs and cast me off it at the precise moment the break began. After a few yards, the wave boiled full around my shoulders and I flailed to keep from being rolled under.

But often I did tumble in briny clouds of churning sand. Instinctively, I held my breath, closed my eyes, pushed my feet against the bottom and blew out as I broke the surface.

I learned to look around as soon as my head was above water, to find my bearings. The shore was constant, solid, a terrestrial North Star. Opposite was the water, dynamic and dangerous, ever-moving.

"Face the breakers or you'll get hit," my daddy said. I could have run to the beach for safety, but he took my hand and we faced the sea.

The deep green beyond the breakers was a club in which my daddy and I were the only members. Swimming in the deep green was like scrambling into a tree house and pulling up the ladder before my mother could enter. In the water, we were bonded by more than blood, and it was only here that we gossiped and told secrets.

His confidences were from a time I considered to be the olden days, when his father and stepmother, Elizabeth, were still alive.

"Once the old man locked me in the car trunk all the way from the volcano to Kona," he told me, his face to the sea. "There wasn't enough room in the seats, and he thought I was a troublemaker. It was that damn Lizzie who caused it all."

My contributions were from the immediate past. "I didn't eat my toast crusts this morning. I threw them in the garbage and Mama didn't see." He made a goofy, upside-down smile.

My daddy's skin was the color of weak coffee. His Hawaiian mother had died when he was a year old. I heard years later that when she lay dead in the front room of the old house in Hilo, Hawaiians came wailing and keening in the ancient, eerie way, despite her haole husband's objections.

In the anguish and upset and trying to provide for her seven young children, no one paid the baby much attention, except his five-year-old sister, Nina. And she cried the loudest when their father shunted the baby to an orphanage for a year. Later, their father packed most of the kids off to board at Kamehameha Schools.

When he finished Kamehameha in 1931, my father moved in "temporarily" with Nina and her husband. He would have stayed longer, but he met my mother on a blind date in 1939 and they married the next year. Just before I was born, they bought a place in Kailua, a small beach house not one hundred yards from the green and untamed waters.

Sometimes on a Sunday, my daddy woke me just before sunrise and we'd shiver our way to the beach as fast as we could walk, hunching our shoulders under thin towels. Then the sun would break the watery horizon, turning the sea luminescent. At that hour, the ocean was always gentle, as if it still slumbered, dreaming of daddies and little girls coming to visit. We waded out to the deep green, where the water, warmer than the air, rose over our shoulders.

Small swells washed over us, glowing gold through green as sunbeams filtered through them in a slow, oceanic hula. The rhythm of the waves was like the repetitive sway of dancers as they reached and bent, telling the story of the chant to the beat of a fish-skin drum. Like the hula, the sea held *kaona*, hidden meanings. My daddy and I didn't talk of "meanings," but I felt graceful and weightless, and I dove a few times, bathing in the dance.

One of these mornings, when we floated in the glowing green, my daddy told me of the *'aumākua*, the personal spirit guardians of Hawaiians. 'Aumākua, he said, often take the form of animals. Ours, he was certain, were creatures of the sea. They watched us always.

But even in our magic, secret green place, that was all my daddy told me about the bond of our people with the sea. He didn't know of the ancient migration voyages from Tahiti and the Marquesas, nor of Kanaloa, the god of the ocean. He didn't even know the names of his Hawaiian grandparents, his haole father having so abruptly severed the family ties. He simply lived what he couldn't explain, his heart's ancient tie with the sea.

Once he set out to accompany my mother and us kids to see my mother's family in North Dakota. But when our steamer docked in San Francisco, the thought of being away from the sea, of being thousands of miles and days of travel away from it, was too much. He waved goodbye to the three of us at the train station.

"I want to go with you!" I cried to my daddy. But Pierre and I went to North Dakota with my mother, and it was months before I returned to my ocean.

In time, I could see that the water was imprinted on my brother, too. As Pierre grew, my daddy taught him to surf. But then came a time when my daddy would rather drink than go to the green water with us. I couldn't understand why.

He became another person entirely. He sat slack in his living room chair, slurring his speech, repeating himself, spilling his highball on his soiled undershirt. Sometimes he came home late at night, loud and stinking, never seeing that my mother had left his share of supper on the stove. Sometimes he didn't come home for days. I hated him. I missed him.

The weaker drink made him, the stronger my mother tried to be. She became the family safety officer, with rules for the beach laid out in detail, owing to the water's clear and present danger. No swimming alone. No one under fourteen to be in the water without an adult present. No board surfing. No one to swim after 4:00 p.m. No one to swim at all if the surf is rough. No swimming in the rain.

Her rules did not forbid walking on the beach. Sometimes Pierre and I returned to the ocean at twilight, when long shadows marked the sand with palm trees and catamaran masts. The light danced obliquely on the water's surface, and the smell of salt wafted heavily on the trade winds. The tide was on its way out again, leaving scalloped rows of tiny shells and bits of seaweed. Incoming tides sometimes brought hand-blown glass fishing floats from Japan that bobbed like big jellyfish on the waves. We walked at water's edge, splashing ankle-deep. Sometimes the ʻaumākua would beckon us too strongly.

"What happened?" our mother screamed when we got home, salt water dripping from our clothes and sand clinging to our wet feet.

"We went swimming."

"In your clothes? After four o'clock? You mustn't!"

But we did. And we did again.

Pierre and I formed an unspoken pact to protect ourselves from the strong, long arm of our mother and the unpredictable drunken outbursts of our father. The water became our haven, and we became its creatures. Sometimes it seemed that Pierre had always been my only companion in the green waters.

•••

Yet every year, once in summer and once right after New Year's, my father went "on the wagon." In a month of no drinking, we'd go to our ocean, as if we had never parted.

Once, more than once, I told him I wanted to be an artist or a writer. He told me more things from the olden days, about how mean Lizzie had been, but how Nina and his other sister sneaked treats to him when he was being punished. He talked of playing football at Kamehameha, coached by Nina's husband, the legendary Doggie Wise. He talked of living with them all those years. And once he said he thought Nina was a fool for divorcing. Yet Nina remained to him as Pierre was to me, the sibling with an unbreakable bond.

When I was just short of sixteen, Nina took to staying with us whenever she came to Oʻahu from the Big Island. She was born on the same date as my mother, and she was, even in midlife, my father's whispering, giggling confidante. Both facts rankled my mother.

One evening Nina said, "I have a schemey idea." She always said "schemey idea." It could be anything—buy shave ice, pick guavas, give the dog a bath. This time she said, "Let's go to the beach."

It was probably 7:30, but midnight-dark. "Oh, no," my mother said. "It's too late."

Nina took it in stride. "OK. We won't be gone long."

She and my father, Pierre and I picked our barefoot way along the coral road that led to the beach. The loose sand felt cool, and we could see bits of waves spitting in the starlight. I was thinking of how it felt to jump in at twilight with all our clothes on when Nina said, "Let's go swimming!"

"We'll all catch hell," my father said.

"Come on, I brought towels. We'll just take our clothes off and run in."

The water was at once the same as always, and altogether different. It was as if I had grown up and my lifetime friend had become my true lover. The breaking surf teased me in the dark to the place I knew was the green, where I couldn't quite touch bottom. The water folded around me, holding me warm in the cool night air, kissing me gently and slowly, combing its wet and reverent fingers through my floating hair. Tiny, tantalizing shivers, shivers I had never felt before, ran up my back. I opened my mouth a little, letting the seawater run in, tasting the salt and feeling the insides of my cheeks with my tongue.

I rose and fell as the swells rolled under me toward shore, and in the hypnotic minutes of the water's night rhythm, I lost the bearings of time. In the dark that was only the sea, I was consumed by a feeling I could call surrender, if ever I had resisted.

Eventually, my mother gave in. Before I left for college, she acknowledged that, although we were hopeless, Pierre and I weren't going to drown.

Fourteen years later, at sixty-one, my father learned at last that alcohol had betrayed him. As he lay in a Honolulu hospital, he schemed for release so he could be near the water of life. One afternoon, as

I leaned over the high hospital bed to kiss his cheek, he whispered so softly I wasn't sure I heard, "I think I'm dying." But he talked the doctors into letting him go home.

In the seaside room of our old house, he lay sober in his own bed, where the waves and the ʻaumākua still called at night. His second night there, he died trying to say something to Pierre and me. The words would not come out, but his mouth started a smile and his eyes opened wide. In my last look into those droopish brown eyes that were so like mine, I saw no weakness or fear, but a happiness I had seen only in the green waters. I knew he had just gone home.

My mother bore no objection to us taking his ashes to the ocean, just as he had taken us so many times. And when she died some years later, her instructions were to scatter her ashes in the waters she had warned us from.

After my father died, Nina couldn't bear to come to the beach. But when she passed on, her grandsons took her ashes to the Kailua waters, too.

Too soon it was Pierre's turn. At forty-two, he lay like our father before him, in the same seaside room, cancer slowly doing its work. The sea breeze rustled the coconut fronds outside, and geckos chirped from the eaves. At night these sounds subsided, and we heard only the tide washing its sandy rhythm, and the ʻaumākua calling.

Once I sat cross-legged on the big bed next to Pierre and asked him, if he had one wish, what would it be?

He knew without thinking. "To go to the water."

On a September Sunday morning, Pierre's wife, their two children and I rose in the dark. A few friends gathered, and we carried to the beach a *pū'olo*, a parcel wrapped in *ti* leaves. The sky was getting light as we arrived. The sea was calm. We waded through the shallows to the deepness of the green, where veins of gold shone in the swells. *To go to the water*, he had said.

We took handfuls of the coarse, gritty ashes from the bundle, and swirled them just beneath the surface, where they spread in the watery glow, indistinguishable from the sand of the ocean floor.

I thought of how the sea with its tides brought things and took them away, and revealed secrets and then covered them again, in its unfailing rhythm. In the green I faced seaward, my nose just above the water, my arms moving just enough to keep me upright. At eye level, the water shimmered, and below its surface it caressed me gently, moving again in the hula. I swam quietly with my family—Pierre, my daddy, Nina and even my dry-land mother. And the 'aumākua and Kanaloa, god of the sea.

One of them, or some of them, or all of them whispered: *I am with you always.*

I was home in the warm suspension of the green waters.

O NOBLE TOOTHBRUSH
2014

I have smashed you flat,
once again splaying bristles
so you look like a string mop
from the Nineteen Forties

Please don't fault me
for worshipping the dental hygienist
who visited our fifth grade class
toting an enormous molar
along with a toothbrush
approaching the size of a baseball bat
exhorting us to brush brush brush
and brush some more

In her name I have so devotedly demolished
the bristles of you and your thousand
predecessors that today's hygienists marvel
at my four shining wisdom teeth
my dentist exonerates me for abusing
you and says to me
You will die with all your teeth in your head

THE WAY BACK
1992

The conch sounds at 5:00 a.m. By starlight I slide from my warm sleeping bag. At the beach the silhouetted *moʻo Lono* silently offers a sip of consecrated water. I step beyond this Hawaiian priest into the dark waters of Kahoʻolawe, a tiny, uninhabited island in the rainshadow of Maui's Haleakalā.

The houses and temples of Kahoʻolawe are ruined, the once-verdant slopes denuded by goats, the soil swirled away by relentless wind and torrential rain, the hardpan surface cratered by fifty years of U.S. Navy live-fire practice bombs. But like Hawaiʻi's aboriginal people, who have endured the cultural battering of two centuries of Western influence, Kahoʻolawe clings to life. I am here as a guest of Protect Kahoʻolawe ʻOhana, a group that has spent two decades healing the island. Though they were branded "radical natives" when they landed on Kahoʻolawe against Navy regulations, five years later their work resulted in the island being added to the National Register of Historic Places. In 1990 the bombing was stopped. As stewards of the island, members of the ʻOhana—

which means "extended family"—have inventoried archaeological sites, built water-catchment systems, and started revegetation projects. Now, in this windy January, the ʻOhana is bringing the ancient annual thanksgiving celebration to a close.

I am a Hawaiian—but, like Kahoʻolawe, tenuously connected to my past. My native grandmother died when my father was a baby, and I grew up knowing little of my culture. Now, submerged in Kahoʻolawe's waters, I follow instructions for the first ceremony: Until the sun rises and the conch sounds again, silently praise Lono, the sustainer of life. Pray for misty rain to nurture Kahoʻolawe with green.

For years I have gone to the sea to meditate at sunrise. I'm suddenly sure that I received the practice from unnamed ancestors who also sought in ritual some sense and order to life. Just then the conch blower, floating far off in the Pacific, lifts his shell horn against the rosy sky.

All morning, people wrap offerings to Lono in ti leaves: banana and sweet potato; taro, redfish and black coconut. At noon a dozen couples line up along the beach wearing white *malo* and *kīkepa*, the loincloth and sarong. Chanting slowly, they bear their bundles to the *imu*, the hot and earthy-smelling cooking pit.

At day's end, two more processions wind to the ruins of the women's and men's temples. In bare feet the Hawaiians feel their way over the lava path, white raiment and Lono banners fluttering. This time the offerings are laid on raised platforms.

The next day we hike the full length of the island, eleven miles under a parching sun. The Navy has cautioned us against picking up anything, because the island is still scattered with unexploded bombs. At mid-island those in the ceremony change into white again and pad barefoot a half-mile off the trail to a promontory where ancient priest-navigators once schooled postulants to read the stars and the currents to sail 2,500 miles back to Tahiti, where the Hawaiians came from a millennium ago. From here I have a clear view of the channel Ke-ala-i-kahiki, the-way-to-Tahiti. The ritual begins. In the gusts we hear only snatches of the chants. Then the final conch blows.

By late afternoon we're blistered, sunburned and dehydrated, but we must reach the western tip of the island before sundown. An hour later we arrive at our destination.

As the celebrants prepare for the final ritual, a regal and massive gray-haired Hawaiian I have not seen before appears. On the sand a hundred feet behind him a four-foot-long scale-model *koa* canoe sits balanced on her outrigger, her *kapa* cloth sail a white triangle in the waning light. For the last time, pairs of Hawaiians make their offerings to the moʻo Lono. Carefully the priests pack the canoe.

At the ocean's edge the chief strikes the waves with a broom of ti leaves. When the surf calms, four of the strongest swimmers guide the canoe toward the channel. The sky fades, and from the shore we can see only the tiny sail, still upright. At last light the canoe catches the current of Ke-ala-i-kahiki, the connection to our ancient homeland.

In the starry night, cold winds blow from both the sea and the land. My skin crinkles with salt. My sleeping bag is damp, but I crawl in and lay my head on a hump of sand. Around me lie other Hawaiians; under me Kahoʻolawe feels alive. I can see the campfire, its flames the shape of the canoe sail, the color of the sunset sky.

EMBERS
FORTY YEARS TOGETHER
2013

You showed me old Basque carvings
In white trunks of golden aspen
Camped with me at the meadows and the lakes
We heard the yodel of the coyotes
You lit a fire in the morning
Had coffee on before I was awake

You taught me to listen
To McKenzie River's music
Row through rocks and rapids on our way
Know the power of the currents
Spot where trout and salmon swim
Sing a song of praise for this one day

Come sit along beside me
Stir the embers of our fire
And remember

We hiked high in your home country
In purple shadows of the Sisters
Bathed ourselves beneath a waterfall
Blooming heather, Johnny-Jump-Ups
Lupine, aster and red paintbrush
Lined our pathways when we heard the call

You said patience is what's needed
To see the yellow harvest moon
And your secret constellation in the sky
We must be quiet this whole evening
Only whisper in the morning
It's easy to do it if you try

You dug out Renfrew Springs once more
Near Gold Hill's old time mines
Huckleberry pancakes in the morn
We camped under our old Big Tree
In the smell of fir and pine
Slept so well we felt we were reborn

Otters played in Emma Lake
We camped at Taylor Burn
Marmots whistled in big rocky slides
A bear had climbed a fir tree
Brandy camp tea after dinner
You told stories in the starry night

We climbed to Lowder Mountain
Cedar swamp and hanging gardens
Glacier lilies popping through the snow

That flat mountain top rolled gently
Like your footsteps always do
Always steady everywhere you go

Now those times are all behind us
Rose alpenglow at sunset
Spreading in our hearts as love and song
We have grown so much together
We know we are forever
In quiet waters where we travel on

Come sit along beside me
Stir the embers of our fire
And remember

BACK TO THE BASTION
1999

The year: 1957. Age: 16. We were junior boarders, about twenty girls hoofing it down the hill to KSB—Kamehameha School for Boys—for Exchange Dinner. The dinner happened but once a year, so we ardently desired to be our most attractive.

In eighth grade, on the sleeping porch in Dorm M at the fortress school on Kapālama Heights, we had pushed all our beds to the window, the better to partake of moonbeams to make us beautiful. As we got older, we taught each other to shave legs, pluck eyebrows and bobby-pin perfect pin curls. For Exchange Dinner, we encased our waists in three-yard skirts and our feet in flats. Some girls even had pink or blue flats.

Anyone knows socks with flats is like wearing a sweatshirt under your prom gown. But just before we left for KSB, the decree came down: It's drizzling. You must wear socks.

Halfway down the switchback walk to Exchange Dinner, we peeled our socks off and stuffed them in the crannies of a stone wall. We showed off our ankles to the boys, then, on our way back up the hill, re-dressed our feet. But for a fink of a chaperone, we would have eluded doom.

Instead, Pink Slips—the paperwork of Detention—and the rolling thunder god-voice of the KSG—Kamehameha School for Girls—principal propelled key phrases into posterity: Painted Hussies! Primordial Skin Sensations!

May detention save our souls.

After four decades, last year I returned to the Victorian bastion for Alumni Week and, a few months later, as writer-in-residence. I trod again upon the very stairs that figured in the crime. In the concrete halls and behind rock walls, phantoms jostled, ghosts of old maid Mainland schoolteachers and widowed housemothers clucked at the new teen girls in their jeans and crop tops peopling the halls as latter-day hussies.

Kamehameha went co-ed in 1965. Now, at *my girls' school*, boys clog the halls and sprawl in the classrooms. The student handbook forbids "displays of affection," but girls twine themselves into the arms of boys sitting on railings. In the name of Old Maid Saints, where are their socks?

I start teaching the first Monday of April in Haleakalā 102, where I had marred my GPA with a C in typing for being fast but rottenly inaccurate. On the *lānai* outside I wrote my first *haiku*, a ditty about a puka in sunset clouds, while I, as dining hall *luna*, waited to ring the chimes calling captive students and teachers to their dinner tables set for eight with knife-fork-spoon and butter spreader.

At each round table sat hostess, waitress, faculty member, and *kuaʻāina* plebes learning to be ladies. The greatest challenge to a hostess: If one person was absent on pie night, she had to cut seven equal pieces.

When the pie was gone and we had placed our napkins to the left of the plate, we sang *a cappella* three-part harmony in that high-ceilinged echo chamber. Often it was "ʻImi Au I Au ʻOe." I Am Searching for Thee. Without socks.

Now the dining hall is the art department and the kids eat in a mayhem cafeteria.

The kids in Haleakalā 102 look so young. Which means I must appear as old as the Pleistocene alumnae who occasionally came as dinner guests to eat an eighth of a pie and listen to "ʻImi Au I Au ʻOe."

Despite today's bare *piko* between crop top and jeans, the kids in Haleakalā were shy. Until the day of the stink fut bridge.

Those foul words—titter, titter, then blatant giggling—came in a recording I played of storyteller Mākia Malo recounting his 1930s Oʻahu childhood. The featured bridge, where Kamehameha Highway plunges through the mangrove swamp near Heʻeia Kea, still stinks.

I uttered "stink fut" myself, thus positioning myself in the same admirable category as writer Rodney Morales, who recently had read on campus the unexpurgated version of his own work and subsequently drew to the English Department a slew of irate phone calls from Mormon mothers.

The day after my stink fut episode, Lois-Ann Yamanaka read to another class from her most recent novel, *Blu's Hanging*. Having been warned of the Morales morality incident, she pointedly censured herself: "'Oh—ah—heck with you,' she said. "'You can just—ah—buzz off.'"

After I brought up the stink fut bridge, the word "crap" escaped my lips once or twice, especially in answer to inquiries about first drafts and writer's block. And, after that, my young charges, their boy hands on girl bodies, their girl socks nowhere to be seen, began to write like real people.

Listen to your Hawaiian heart, I told them. Listen to the *'āina*. Life is made up of relationships, of dualities. Our ancestors composed chants about all this, in layers of metaphor. Write, now, in English, about your name, your home, about being Hawaiian. Write a gift for someone. Talk to an older person and get him or her to tell you a story. Every day, sit outdoors and be quiet, and make an entry in your 'Āina Journal.

> *4/8/99 as I sit on the damp porch I carefully listen to the music of the rain. I hear the rhythm of the rainfall ... Nature's percussion beating down on the earth, leaving pieces of heaven here to remain. I glance at my neighbor's shingled roof and see the rainwater cascade in deliberate successions. A single raindrop comes to the end of*

its journey as it falls from the heavens, rolls down the roof and nestles in the yearning land.
—Jordan Lee

At the end of nine class sessions, ninety-three students turned in twenty-four pounds of writing. I read my way through the stacks for more than a week.

Some of the writing came computer-printed, some scrawled in pink tinsel ink. Ekona Ravey wrote about his Hawaiian name entirely in Hawaiian. I stared. I marveled.

Some of these kids have taken Hawaiian language for five years. In my dad's day, the school forbade students to speak Hawaiian. In my day, we studied Hawaiian for six weeks of seventh and eighth grade.

Even in Abraham Pi'ianaia's eighth grade class, we never got past parts of the body. *Maka, pepeiao, papalina.* Eye, ear, cheek. *Ihu, waha, pu'uwai.* Nose, mouth, heart.

One day Mr. Pi'ianaia gave an oral quiz.

"The word for toe?" He pointed at Marcella Choy.

Marcella was both ignorant and impish: "To'e," she piped.

I studied Ekona's upright black calligraphic letters forming a perfect square block on a lined notebook page, like a tablet of runes made of vowels and diacritical marks. I marveled again. And wept, for I could not read it.

I discovered that some students staunchly favor sovereignty. Others are flatly opposed.

One wrote that "Hawaiʻi was an independent nation a long time ago, the 1940s to be exact," but it was overthrown in the 1950s and became a U.S. state.

I started to chuckle at the date errors, but the kid was more informed than I at the same age. In the mid-fifties, just before Hawaiʻi became a state, we knew mainly that our buildings were named for dead chiefs of a dead kingdom. Except the KSG library. William O. Smith was an original Bishop Estate trustee.

Twenty years later, I discovered that he also was Lorrin Thurston's right-hand man in overthrowing the Kingdom of Hawaiʻi.

In Dorm L at the alumni reunion—I mean Kinaʻu Hale, because the school likes being Hawaiian now—I take comfort in familiarity. Yeah, there's a smoke detector in my room, and carpet on the floor. But a desk still stands in front of three-paned brass-framed windows that crank outward over the half-round Spanish tiles of the lānai roof below. How many times did we shine these windows by pasting them with Bon Ami and wiping it off with newspaper?

I'm thinking: These dorms—built about 1930 of stuccoed lava rock—are designed for ventilation. Unceasing wind blows into the *mauka* rooms, through the hallway via screened transoms, and out the windows of the *makai* rooms. It's June, but so cool I crank the windows shut. And for the first time—it wasn't allowed in ancient days—I pull up the sliding wood panel to cover the screen on my door to the hallway. Suddenly the truth comes to me: Ventilation, my butt. These dorms were designed for housemother surveillance.

My neighbor sharing the room-connecting sink—What? You went to class and left a spot of water on the faucet? Detention!—whispers, lest her secret float over the transom, that a "girl" from the Class of '53 has come to board for Alumni Week with her boyfriend even though she has a husband. Shh. She's only one floor beneath us.

At the opening Alumni Reception, the Reunion Gestapo chastises me for cutting off my Reunion ID Bracelet, the kind you get in a hospital. I'm too old for detention.

In seventh grade, my friend Jackie never got to go home to Pearl City one single Saturday from Labor Day to Thanksgiving because of detention. Wastepaper in the wastebasket. Wrinkle in the bedspread. Towels folded without name tag showing. Worst of all, lipping off to the housemother. Dorm advisors, they call them now.

The regimental days are gone. Nobody cares if you stay up late, or if you don't wash your comb and hairbrush on Thursday, or if the seven school dresses in your closet face the same way. Actually, girls now don't even wear dresses.

But boarding kids today—now a much smaller proportion of the whole student body—still long for home.

Tangible
A long road up the mountain
A tedious journey indeed,
A reward awaits my soul.
The closer I get
The more steps I take
The journey to recleanse my soul.
Home provides mana
Home instills tranquility
Home is where I belong.
Makawao.
—Gina Kekiwi

Affluence—some kids live in condos with swimming pools instead of plantation huts, many travel across the United States and even overseas instead of over the Koʻolau Mountains—can't change the eternal: contending with parents, wishing for a prom date, being thrilled with seeing your breath the first time you go to a cold place.

Or racism.

One time I was in California and these guys thought I was Mexican and they called me names. I didn't like that. They couldn't tell that I was part white and part Hawaiian. There is nothing wrong with Mexicans but if they were going to call me something I rather have them call me something that I was.
—Melanie Park

from "A Gift"

To my parents I'll give this
for thanks long overdue.
Through all the pain and trouble
You're always there to help.
Let's not forget cash.

I may think I know all
but daily I need your help
Problems with life and school
Questions about my future
And how to get to the theater.

You give me so much freedom
I often take advantage of it
I'm lucky that I'm last
You don't let me forget that
Thanks for giving me the car tonight.

You've always trusted me
and believed I'd do good
and I usually do, as much as I can
because you give me that trust
I don't have a curfew, do I?

—Jess Kaneshiro

Where are all the other K names? Kahapea, Kaialoa, Kamaunu? Kaupiko, Kaupu, Keanu? The rolls have gone to Fujita, Castro, Todorovich. Where once a quarter Hawaiian was the minimum blood requirement, these kids rattle lists of a dozen bloods in their veins. For many, Hawaiian is the last microscopic ingredient, like "natural vitamin E to preserve freshness."

I ask my students to gather stories from *kūpuna*. Many of them talk with grandparents who are Chinese, Filipino or Japanese. Kevin Fong's grandfather fought in Europe in World War II with the famous AJAs of the 442nd Regimental Combat Team and the 100th Battalion.

My elder

He and a bunch of his buddies went out to a restaurant to eat. They had this steak meal for $1.75, a dollar seventy-five. Then it comes time to tip. Most people are leaving tips like 25 cents so they're throwing down $2. But my grandpa folks throw down $5. That makes a $3.25 tip, almost enough for two more steak meals. The waitress' eyes got as wide as saucers. She swore my grandpa folks were mad and threatened to call the police. But they were sober and sane.
They were stationed there for two weeks and they ate out quite often. At all the restaurants they ate, had a good time and left a 300 percent tip. Everywhere they went people thought they were mad, insane, crazy, loony, this band of Nisei Japanese men. But word of their generosity got out and they were met with great hospitality and care. My grandpa and his band had changed New Yorkers' feelings toward Japanese.

—Kevin Fong

Ikaika Enos took to heart my ranting about looking for dualities, and metaphorical meaning in names.

My name is Lanikeha. I am everything people fear. I am everything people love. I am a changeling. I am sixteen years old. I am four years old. I am eighty years old. My name is Ikaika. I am strong. I am weak. I am outspoken, yet meek. I am a fading blossom. I am a budding rose. Maybe I'm the thorns also. Yes, I'm the thorns too.

I am the root of many. I am the branch of many trees. I nourish. I eradicate. I am fertilizer, I am poison.

My name is Kūkaʻilimoku. I am what you fear. I am what you need. I sustain, I destroy. I create, I obliterate. I am shelter. I am your baby blanket, your teddy bear. I am the boogeyman. The monster underneath your bed is my cousin.

My name is Lebraun. It's French for gentle power. No one besides my daddy calls me Lebraun. I am protective. It is my solace. I am secretive. I have to be. I am resilient. I am thick-skinned. I am dark and cold.

I am predictable. I am unpredictable. My name is Kalaniʻanaʻole. No, I'm not named after that damn highway. I am rich. I am poor. I am evasive. I'm the best liar you've ever known. I am a master of manipulation. I am evocative. I am precious.

I am Hawaiian. I am Portuguese and German and Irish. I am proud. Damn proud. I will never back away. I will never stray away. I will never run away.

I am invincible. I am fragile. I love. I hate. I cry. I laugh, I enjoy, I covet. I breathe. I bleed. I envy. I am what you have seen, what you hope to see, what you hate to feel, what you need to survive. I am who I am.

—Ikaika Enos

I hear stories, I tell stories. I steal stories, I deal stories. I am a pipeline. I am a gossip. I find out what's happened in fifty years to my own classmates.

Ti flies stand-by, with no itinerary. She's prone to get lost, which she especially likes in England, where "some kind young person" takes her by the shoulders to turn her in the right direction and calls her "Love." She wants to make three more trips to England so she can be lost in the whole country.

Toomey travels to the Mediterranean and Europe with a minute-by-minute itinerary she thinks will prevent her being mugged, robbed, accosted, kidnapped, raped or hijacked.

She is husband-hunting for her kid sister, Carol, who is only fifty-six or so. At our hen party, Toomey learns the six-second stare technique from Wendy. Look into a stranger's eyes for six seconds and SMILE.

He'll come and ask you something. Toomey plans to do this, but she'll duck so the guy will go for Carol.

One evening Rosemary busts out of our seated-only hula training. The more she dances—on her feet, using, gasp, her hips—the more dollar bills flutter at her feet. A one-time football player throws all his credit cards. Then he flings his whole wallet. A measly former tennis player—who's been monitoring snoring in the dorms and so is awake at night anyway—pitches his room key. Ha-ha, we're too old for detention.

Lūʻau the last night. We're told it's not "lūʻau," it's "ʻahaʻāina," a new old word. The school likes being Old Hawaiian now.

Getting ready is a reprise of graduation afternoon, too excited to rest, gathering in the room that has the most contraband crackseed and sushi, wearing robes and pj's and *pareu*. Worrying that a lei is not the right color for a *muʻumuʻu*. Worrying that we'll sweat and smell stink. Worrying that we won't take our glasses and then we'll have to read something.

ʻĀina journal 4/11/99

It's still all right here. I guess there's too much buildings here. But at least you can still see the beauty of the land sometime. It's like our people. We're a minority in our own land. We're the mountains in the back behind of all the buildings. We're here but no one notices us. We're here that's all. I'm telling you, the mountains the ocean they are forever. The buildings will fall.

—Ekona Ravey

One student writes that "darkness is an interesting devil." Another calls the North Star the "Star of Wisdom."

Perhaps wisdom will come from some of these young hussies and their boyfriends.

My last day with my ninety-three kids—they are my kids, after two weeks—I answer questions and tell writer stories. And then I walk alone on the covered sidewalk where I was busted once for kissing at Sunday afternoon "calling." Today, in the same spot, a boy nuzzles a girl's neck. Kiss-kiss. Kiss some more.

I walk by them to the parking lot, and then motor down the hill. The bastion of Kapālama reels by in the rearview mirror like forty years of movie. In a freeze-frame, the painted hussies paint themselves into the scene. *Déjà vu.*

TEACUPS AND DOLLS
2014

I have dusted
seventy years, since
I was the perfect size
to run a piece of retired cotton shirt
over the oak claw feet
of Grandma's dining table

Now my knees say
crawling's not so easy
but upright I have come to see
the Zen of dusting

Handblown glass
fishing floats my friend
Gena found on her wild beach
as imperfect and beautiful
under my cloth as Gena
with her frickin'-ass
mouth and true devotion
to the movie green guy Shrek

Bone China tea cups
all I have of my other
grandmother dead thirty
years before my birth
I hold her cup, dusting,
wondering if her fingers,
like mine, were too big
for the delicate handle

I dust my own
Raggedy Ann and Andy
shocked that my childhood
harbored today's antiques
dust Pocket Doll, my daughter's
pal some forty years ago
now aiming for relic status too

I use a little lemon oil
on the miniature outrigger
canoe my father claimed
he made, but anyone
knows he sat with bourbon
in hand while
his woodworker brother
carved a chunk of koa

I'm glad dust steals
through our aging
double-hung windows
otherwise I would not know
my dusting works just like
walking meditation

ALOHA, OJIBWA
1997

It's a Sunday, the Kaministikwia River drifting wide and gentle past the front gate of Ontario's Old Fort William. Inside the palisades, on a dampish patch of lawn, fifteen men and women sit cross-legged on a circle of Hudson's Bay blankets. They have just begun the Ojibwa purification ceremony at Keeshigun, the annual Ojibwa weekend celebration at this living history fur trade-era fort in Canada.

I had come the day before, a writer on vacation, peeking two hundred years into the past. I live in Oregon, thousands of miles from Ontario, equally far from my Hawaiian ancestors' Pacific homeland, where I was born and schooled. Today I have returned to Old Fort William, thinking to catch the canoe-building demonstration, to converse with voyageurs and clarks.

The dance ground of the day before, where I had seen a regal man in purple and a younger Ojibwa in striking black and white, lies quiet in the early morning. On the nearby lawn, slightly inside the blanket circle, a small woman intones something too softly for me to hear. I step closer. A man beckons me to the one remaining seat on the grass. I sit, remove my sandals. What to do now? I had meant to be an observer. To my left sits the purple warrior from the dance, now wearing jeans and a crumpled white shirt. Before him on the ground, grasses smolder in an abalone shell. He whooshes the smoke over his head, around his body. Then he whispers to me: "Remove your jewelry to smudge."

My insides churn like the volcanic middle earth, reminding me how I hate well-meaning but ignorant strangers appropriating my people's ceremonies, how I despise arrogant tourists denigrating our ancient gods. What to do? Clearly the warrior expects me to "smudge."

My rings stick. I lick my finger, force the first ring over my knuckle. The bowl of smoke passes around the entire circle clockwise, back to me. I don't know what to do. I look to my new friend. He just nods. I lean over, inhaling cautiously. To my surprise, the smoke is calming. I turn my hands over it, as if drying them. I waft the smoke toward my face. I hand the bowl to my friend. It feels like a chalice.

The bowl passes back to the elder leading the group. She smudges last, "as a sign that no one is better than any other." Those who are Christian, she says, may recite the Lord's Prayer in Ojibwa. A few people do. She opens the circle to other prayers, exhorts us to include all people in our supplications, tells us that's why Indians refer to four colors, for all the people of the Earth. She says it is up to us to set things right.

In the silence, an ax splitting firewood rings out from across the fort's main square. To my right, a white man prays for the black birch dying from acid rain. A woman across the circle confesses how embarrassed she is to be white, how she carries the sins of the fathers. My friend on my left prays: "I thank the Great Spirit for the gift of sight to see the beauty of the Earth, for the gift of smell … the gift of hearing … I thank the Great Spirit for the privilege of having a family to care for."

To me his English words from his Ojibwa heart are like new fire under a full kettle. I think of how I renounced Christianity long ago, of meeting an old Mohawk chief some years later. He looked at me carefully and said, "What are you? I see in your eyes that you must go back to your people." Now, at words from another Indian, the reservoir that is my heart bursts. My eyes fill with tears. My nose begins to drip, but I dare not wipe it. And then, almost choking, I do something I have not done since I was a Sunday school child: I pray by myself out loud. "I pray for my people," I begin, choking, "who are Hawaiian. I pray for my people, who are the people of all the Earth. I pray that we let the Earth heal us, that we in turn might heal the Earth." I have finished. I try not to sniffle.

The elder looks up. "Thank you," she says. "Thank you." She and two young Indian men flanking her take up rattles, and sing in Ojibwa. The ceremony is over.

My new friend, the purple warrior, speaks. Vernon Kimball, a name as Indian as mine is Hawaiian, a name because our grandmothers or our grandmothers' grandmothers married the white men who came to their lands. Vernon wants to know about Hawaiians. I tell him how I go home twice a year to learn, to write about my people. He asks if I would speak a few words at the dancing in the afternoon. I am a writer, not a speaker. I sweat fear, thinking about how large the crowd was yesterday. Hundreds, maybe a thousand. I swallow hard, and I think, "No." And then I hear myself say, "Of course."

In the afternoon the sun beats down and the drums begin. Six singers wail in a center shade pavilion. Dancers of America's first nations wind around the circle in waving ranks, moccasined toes keeping the rhythm, point-step, point-step. I am squeezed among the spectators. Around the curve comes the young man I saw yesterday in the dance with Vernon. Three-fourths of his face is painted white. His long black hair flows over his white bone breastplate. Eagle feathers on his head and back fan with power, black leggings striped with white.

Vernon steps out of the dance, leans toward me and says, "Come." I follow. He introduces me to the announcer, who says, "In five minutes, at the end of this song."

Vernon takes my hand and lays it open. "I have the traditional gift for you." He lays a large pinch of tobacco in my palm, and slides back into the dance. The tobacco is a light rusty brown, fine in texture. I close my hand over it and with my fist I press a little writing tablet against my leg. With my other hand I write some notes. My pen struggles. What will I say? My handwriting careens nervously over the small page. I hear my name on the speakers. My heart thumps like the drums, my perspiring hand clutches the tobacco.

"Aloha. I am native Hawaiian." My voice comes from the speakers slowly, clearly. I feel like I have unwrapped in front of the whole world a secret I should never have kept. People listen. "I bring greetings to all of you and especially the Ojibwa and other nations, from the aboriginal people of our Islands in the middle of the Pacific Ocean. We share a similar history of losing our traditional lands. We also share a similar commitment to regaining and perpetuating our culture."

My scrawly notes look to me like someone else wrote them. But I know the voice I hear is mine. "One hundred fifty years ago our king gave us the words that are now the state motto: *Ua mau ke ea o ka ʻāina i ka pono*. The life of the land shall flourish when all is set to rights."

I hand back the microphone and stand beside the emcee. The drums resume. And out of the dancers comes the young man in black and white. He takes my hand, holds on to it, locks his eyes into mine. "I shall always remember your words," he says. "Thank you."

The announcer thanks me, the elder from the purification ceremony thanks me. Vernon thanks me. I walk away, sit on a wooden box to recover. Again,

I fight tears. I am proud of myself, a native person standing among other native people, standing to be counted.

But I must do something with Vernon's tobacco, now sculpted by sweat and shaped by the life line of my hand. I sit on the box, my tobacco hand as useless as if it were in a sling. I cannot throw this gift away. I must honor its sacred meaning. In a few moments it comes to me: I'll wrap the tobacco and take it home, to offer it to Pele, our goddess of the volcano. I'll offer it for all of us trying to keep our heritage alive as we face the turn of another century. To Hawaiians, Pele is the literal, fiery force that destroys the old land and builds the new. To me she also is the symbol of my people's rebirth, and of mine, as we rise from the shards of our shattered culture. From Pele's ever-dynamic work is formed the Earth.

I fetch a paper towel from the ladies' room, carefully wrap the tobacco in it and walk down the path that leads out of Fort William along the wide and gentle Kaministikwia River, down the path that leads from this land of strong and gentle warriors to my homeland in the middle of the Western sea.

MOTHER'S NIGHT
2004

My most important Mother's Day happened at night. It was not even the second Sunday in May, but a June Wednesday, 1988.

My son, Rolf Moan, had graduated from college the year before and was renting a house in Kāneʻohe with his older sister. I happened to be their houseguest. Tamara, as always, had given me a present on official Mother's Day, but as always, the date had escaped Rolf. One year he had sent me a Mother's Day gift in September.

On this June day, Rolf came home from work last, around 5:30 p.m. Tamara and I were in the kitchen pondering dinner.

"Hey, hey, hey," he announced. "Get your swimsuits and your towels. It's Mother's Night!"

We zipped to Kailua, to my sister-in-law's house at the beach, grabbed the community-property Boogie boards, and hit the sand.

We scanned the perfect surf, splashed out past the break line, then hurtled side by side on the first good wave, calling out, "Race! Race!"

At the end of each ride, we grabbed our boards and ran back through the surf, until we began to shiver in the purple shadows of the last of the windward twilight. My sister-in-law stood on the beach in a sweatshirt like a sensible person, taking pictures. She said we looked like three kids, which I took as a compliment.

We showered at her house, Rolf bought dinner at a Kailua deli, then tickets for the new movie *Good Morning, Vietnam*. We finished the evening with mango ice cream cones.

Mother's Night had been glorious, but it's taken me more than fifteen years to understand why I can still conjure vividly that particular tingle of the twilight on my skin, the sound of Robin Williams shouting, "Good morning, Viet-NAM!" and that slick creamy mango taste.

That night was a turning point. Not a sharp-cornered soda cracker turn, but a smooth Saloon Pilot transition around the edge of a circle. For one thing, it ended my societal celebratory expectations. Mother's Day didn't have to be on the second Sunday of May. I could have a surprise Mother's Night any time of year and love it!

Better still, since then I have stood—or surfed, as the case may be—not with my children, but with my two utterly best friends. I know deep in my motherly bones that on the first Mother's Night, the three of us rounded the last part of that long, slow, Saloon Pilot curve and slid into a time of total friendship.

It had been brewing ever since Tamara was born. Two and a half years later, Rolf arrived. In no time, Tom, their dad, had them throwing balls, swinging bats and reciting his mantra, "Keep your eyes on the ball." I taught them Pete Seeger protest songs, covered them in old-shirt smocks, and put paints, brushes and paper on a garage-sale table that became the center of their "art room."

When Rolf was four, having been told that when he grew up he could be anything he wanted, he declared he would be a kangaroo.

Before long, they were spending their afternoons decking themselves in old costumes. They repaired to the art room and created hand puppets (and libretto) for their own opera, *Piggaletta*. They interviewed their father on tape for their homemade radio program, and published a newspaper, *The Sunday Slush*, circulation six.

They both continue to write. But it was turning that Saloon Pilot "corner" that has allowed us to critique each other's work. This is the first essay I've written in more than a decade that hasn't passed their eyes and been enhanced by their suggestions. At the turn of the century, we even began a monthly critique group, and last Christmas self-published a few copies of our best stories and poems.

The first hint of working together came a year before the inaugural Mother's Night. Their dad had died—Tom and I had divorced years earlier—and we wrote a three-part essay about him for *Single Dad* magazine.

In 1990, Tamara and I enrolled in the Port Townsend Writers' Conference in Washington state. When another conference participant mistook us for sisters, we decided to play to the crowd. Our white lie lasted several days.

Tamara, an artist, also extracted a promise from me that, in our free time, we would paint watercolors every day. In turn, I got her to help me with a photographic engineering project. On the beach in Port Townsend, she took my picture with a toy sailboat Rolf had given me for—guess what?—Mother's Night. The trick was to position the toy boat in the extreme foreground and me yards beyond, so Rolf could plainly see I had sailed on his boat. I had to stand thigh-deep in bone-warping cold water, but it was worth it.

Of course we drew some stares, but *c'est la vie*. We'd suspected for years we'd had too many whiffs of Goof Gas, a medical phenomenon we learned about by watching *The Adventures of Rocky and Bullwinkle*.

For Rolf's thirtieth birthday, I made him a Goof Gas Gun, a double-barreled affair fabricated of the finest cardboard tubes, the barrels burnished with silver spray paint. He hung it on his law office wall.

He developed a theory that someday the three of us would all be the same age. At first I thought he was suffering from Goof Gas again, but then I remembered what Tamara had told me around my thirty-fifth birthday when I was pitching a fit about Getting Old.

She was thirteen. "Don't be so silly," she said. "It's only the way we count. It has nothing to do with how old you really are."

I never had another birthday trauma. And now I think Rolf's theory has proved out.

Sometimes the three of us rise in the dark and scuttle to Kailua Beach to watch the sun come up. Goof Gas must need warmth to generate its wonders, because it is never present in these chilly dawn pilgrimages. In fact, if we have to speak, we feel compelled to whisper.

As I sit snuggled silently against my companions on the cold, damp sand, my mind often conjures once again the magic of Mother's Night, and I feel exactly what Rolf wrote in his critique of one of my poems:

"It makes me mysteriously happy."

And for this most glorious of all blessings, I salute my children and best friends, Tamara and Rolf Moan.

GIFTS FROM THE SEA
2007

One morning a soggy
tennis ball
the next evening
a partly husked
coconut
then a perfect
stick
a week later
the prize of all, a dead
fish

Not what I have in mind
a rare purple cowry shell
or handblown fishing float
but surely a dog's best
dreams come true

VOICE OF THE BELOVED
2002

The morning Kū and Hina joined, I knelt in the low-tide, reef-protected shallows of Mokulēʻia, sandals cast onto the dry sand and skirt hiked up around my hips. My inappropriate dress testified that I had not expected an encounter with the ocean—or with a gourd, or with "Mama," *kupuna* Betty Jenkins' ninety-year-old mother, Elizabeth Ellis.

Nor was I thinking of the progenitor Hawaiian gods, the archetypal male and female. My purpose was to learn more about the kupuna role at the Office of Hawaiian Affairs. Aunty Betty had invited me to a cultural workshop for OHA staff members she was holding at her beachside home. I expected motivation and morale building. You know, a pep talk about the good of the organization, the glory of being a corporate cog.

I had met the gracious Aunty Betty once before, so I should have known there would be a twist. Should have known my status as observer would last barely minutes.

The first clue was her home's name: Kai Hāwanawana. Whispering sea. Then I spotted thirty or so dry-but-dirty gourds sitting on her rain-washed lawn.

"*Nānā ka maka,*" Aunty Betty said to twenty assembled employees and me. "Look at these *ipu*. They have had a hard life. They've been exposed to rain and sun, and they are covered with dirt and mold. But listen to them. One will call to you. Do not pick one up and put it down to choose another. Let one call. *Ho'olohe.* Obey."

When nearly everyone else had taken one, I walked slowly to the band of gourds. Of the remaining eight, one with a fat neck seemed like a child in need of love. I picked it up.

"*Ho'oma'ema'e ma ke kai,*" Aunty Betty said. Time for cleansing in the sea.

We walked our gray and dismal gourds down a slope of coarse coral sand. I strapped my watch to my tank top, hitched up my skirt and knelt at the water's edge, following instructions with the others, scouring the scum from my ipu with *limu* and sand.

All the ipu began to shine, hidden beauty of gold and brown coming out as if it were the kaona, the veiled meaning, of a Hawaiian chant or song. Women called to each other, holding their gourds up and turning them. "Look! Nice, yeah?"

I worked and worked in the oblique morning sun, the quiet water lapping, whispering. *Kai hāwanawana.* I scrubbed away at the bottom, the rounded sides, the neck, around the stem as withered as a baby's umbilical cord ready to fall off.

When we finished, we walked back to the house.

"How beautifully we shine when someone cares for us," Aunty Betty said. "Keep listening to your ipu. It will tell you its name."

I listened as I took my *ipu* through the next steps. *Ka ʻoki ana*. Cut the neck. *Hoʻomaʻemaʻe naʻau*. Clean the inside, the guts. But save the seeds.

The neck was big enough that I could get my hand inside the gourd. I pulled at its dusty, dried fibers. I think I heard a small whisper, like the whisper of the sea, perhaps the rattle of seeds still bound in stringy membrane within. The voice said, "*Pilialoha*." Beloved.

I thumped the gourd's bottom to loosen the last seeds. The sound was firm, mellow.

"Nice sound," another woman said. "*Ka Leo*," I thought. The Voice. The next step was *Hāʻawi inoa i ka ipu*. Naming the gourd.

With a formal title for the process, I knew this wasn't the time to casually write a word on the bottom of the gourd with a Magic Marker. The name would bring *mana*, the life force, living power.

"I'm ready," I said to Aunty Betty.

"Talk to Mama," she said.

Mama sat in the house, a tiny wisp of a Chinese-Hawaiian woman in a soft muʻumuʻu. I knelt at her side with the shining, golden gourd, fearing my paltry knowledge of Hawaiian language might be so inadequate I would accidentally give my gourd a name with a hidden meaning of darkness.

"What name do you think?" Mama said.

"Pilialoha. It is from the name of my home, *Hale Pilialoha.*"

"Beloved," Mama said. "A good name."

"I think there's more. More came to me." I paused. I wasn't sure of my Hawaiian grammar. Maybe the rest was too stupid, or simple, or presumptuous. "Ka Leo," I said. "May I call it Kaleopilialoha?" Had I really heard these words or were they wishful thinking? My heart thumped beneath my ribs as if it were inside the gourd. I did not want to be dubbed a fool.

"Yes," Mama said, her gentle, milky old eyes looking right into mine. "Yes, that is good. The Voice of the Beloved."

Aunty Betty had said the ancient people used gourds for dozens of purposes, to store things, to carry water, to keep the cadence. Are we not like gourds, to serve many purposes? Must we not cleanse ourselves inside and out to be able to do our work? When we have done all this in the right order, must we not be beautiful? The corporate pep talk was over.

The next morning I took Kaleopilialoha to the beach of my own babyhood, to the morning surf of Kailua. We sang together, Kaleo and I, knee-deep in the chop and backwash of the incoming tide, chanting what Aunty Betty had taught:

E hō mai
E hō mai
E hō mai ka ʻike mai ē

O na mea huna noʻeau o na mele ē
E hō mai
E hō mai
E hō mai ka ʻike mai ē.

Guide us from above. Help us to know the hidden meaning of the chant. Thump-thump, thump thump thump, Kaleo kept the cadence. I splashed the gourd with water. The sea, or the sky, or the spirits compelled me to talk to it.

You were born in salt water, as was I. You seem to be male, for I am female. We are all both male and female, Kū and Hina. I am the Path of the Rainbow, Keala-o-Ānuenue. But I must also be you, a voice. You were born yesterday, Kaleopilialoha, at Mokulēʻia. Today I honor you at my own beloved Kailua. You shall give full voice to *E Hō Mai*. Guide us from above. Show us the hidden meaning of the chant.

Here I was, talking to a gourd, but I didn't care if people taking their morning beach walk thought I was *lōlō*.

I remembered kai hāwanawana, the whispering sea. At the end of the morning at Mokulēʻia, Aunty Betty had hugged me. "I see that you got it," she said. She held me at arm's length, smiling. And she whispered, like the sea, "The gourd is you."

A CLOSING CONVERSATION
1987

"It's worse than we thought," the surgeon said. "I had hoped there would be two or three tumors and we could put in bypasses. But these things are just all over the large bowel." He looked among us for comprehension.

"I'm sure the lab work will show this is pancreatic cancer. I'd say Tom has two or three months at most." He paused again. "Then again, one of these could rupture…"

I had been with Tom three hours earlier. I offered to leave while a nurse shaved his torso. He said, "No, please stay. You've seen me before."

Not for many years, I thought.

I walked alongside the gurney, holding his hand. The elevator's double doors opened, he to go one way to surgery and I the other. I kissed his cheek, and he mine. The nurse had no idea our marriage had ended twelve years before.

In all that time the only thing we ever had discussed was the kids. Soon the oldest would graduate from college.

Now I said, "I'll be here when you come out."

I stepped into the hallway that may as well have been in the bowels of an unfamiliar ship. I lurched as though the steamer were pitching and rolling, and my vision blurred as tears washed over my eyes like storming seas against a porthole.

The surgeon's news was everything I had hoped not to hear. I stood up, still feeling the roll of that ship. I went home to call the kids. When I got back to the hospital, Tom was in his bed again, imprisoned in medical paraphernalia. His eyes were closed, and sweat beaded his brow.

As I seated myself next to the intravenous carrier and looked at him so pale, exhausted and vulnerable, memories flashed in my head as half-second frames of a movie starring us. He was a blond baseball player with a big brain. I was a girl who hated shoes and was feisty with female independence. We'd met in college when we were scarcely more than twenty, at the height of our idealism, and we married not long after, convinced we would be "free spirits" together forever.

Twelve years was all we could muster.

Now the robust six-footer barely made a lump under the sheet. I wiped the sweat from his head with the corner of a Kleenex. I could not for the life of me recall why our marriage had gone sour.

He opened his eyes. "Hi," he said. His voice sounded just like he looked, tiny and bone-weary.

"Can I have some water?"

I could feel my emotional reservoir fill beyond capacity. The overflow flooded out my eyes.

"Oh, I'm sorry," I said. "I can't seem to keep from crying." He always had hated displays of emotion, crying most of all.

"That's OK," he replied weakly. "This is a sad time." He grimaced, as a woman in labor. "I didn't think there would be so much pain," he whispered. "It arcs over me like a searing light so bright you can't look at it."

After a time the nurses came with another dose of Demerol, and he rested more easily. When he woke again, he was more alert.

Now, I thought, and I opened my mouth.

"I hope you know," I said, and began again to weep. He patted my hand. I swallowed. "That I have long since forgiven you for any real or imagined transgressions." Now tears cascaded, and my eyes began to burn. "I hope that's the case vice-versa."

"Oh, yes," he said. "Long ago."

I sucked in a deep breath. I had just one more thing to get out. "I loved you a lot," I said. "I guess I still do."

"Those feelings don't just go away," he replied.

The kids, Tom's sister and his brother and sister-in-law all arrived in time for the good days. Tom went for hall walks with us, wheeling the IV contraption and the urine bag.

One day I came and the IV was gone. So were the drain tube and the catheter. Tom was ordering strawberry Jell-O and beef stew, watching the Boston Celtics on TV, and reminiscing with his sister about childhood pranks. Yet the whites of his eyes were yellow with foreboding.

I could feel myself draining. My shoulders were a mass of knots, my lower back a study in tension.

At home I invented "therapeutic housework" to keep my hands occupied while my mind ran rampant over unconscious selections from the past, the unbelievable reality of the present and the certainty of the immediate future.

By day Tom was lucid. By night the boundaries blurred between what we consider to be reality and the dreamland of another dimension. The hospital allowed family to stay overnight in Tom's room. So we knew of his sleep talk, of visions of water to cross, of plans for running, of the necessity of "having to go." One night he sat bolt upright and acted out all the roles in Custer's Last Stand.

To our son it was bizarre. To Tom's sister it was a retreat to a childhood of watching cowboy movies at the local theater every Saturday morning. To me he was getting ready, testing the waters of another world.

I do not hold specific religious beliefs, but as I watched him day by day, I became convinced that another dimension does exist, and I feared not that he would die, but only that he would suffer too long. Perhaps the other dimension took hold of me, too, for I lost my earthly sense of time. It was hard to remember what day it was, or whether Tom had been in the hospital two weeks or three. And was it only a month ago he had been out playing golf? How could this disease take him so fast?

In another day or two I would wish the cancer to race on faster through his pain, to propel him into peace. His dying was at once much too fast and entirely too slow, and my mind wallowed in its own confusing new dimension, in need of a worldly anchor

We spoke for the last time two days before he died. The previous Wednesday had been the end of his reprieve. He had vomited suddenly, bursting some of his stitches, losing his oral pain medication, catapulting into all-encompassing pain. He gasped in panic for hours as a new tumor squeezed his windpipe. For the time being he slept, cradled by morphine, weary from enduring and from radiation to keep the new tumor at bay.

Suddenly his eyes popped open and he was fully alert. He even smiled. He looked right at me and said, "Two to five days."

"How do you know? Did a doctor say so?"

He cocked his head and tapped his temple with his forefinger.

I considered his news. "I'm glad you were a big part of my life," I whispered.

"Me, too," he said. "Me, too." He squeezed my hand weakly and smiled the kind of tiny smile babies do sometimes when they have a little gas bubble. Then he slipped back into the haze.

The day he finished dying was a Sunday, one month exactly since he had entered the hospital.

I stood at his window, parting the curtains with my hands to gaze idly on an intersection I had passed hundreds of times. The Dairy Queen reigned on one corner, the Peking Mandarin cheap Chinese joint opposite. I was only five floors up, but I beheld the scene as if from a DC-10 at 35,000 feet. The street looked flat, small, unfamiliar, more like a diagram or a map. I wasn't sure I ever had walked there.

The family and close friends had assembled around Tom's bed. The doctor held Tom's wrist gently, monitoring the fading pulse and listening to the slow, irregular breathing that dominated the room the way a whisper echoes in an old-fashioned library. At last another breath did not come, and the doctor looked up and nodded.

Later I went back into the room. Tom's body lay just as he had for days. But it looked much smaller, and he clearly wasn't in it. Yet I still could feeling him close by. I addressed myself to his body, for lack of seeing where else he was.

"It's OK," I said. "It's really OK to die." I touched his arm softly.

"Goodbye," I whispered, as if trying not to wake him.

As in one of those rare moments when the sun shines while it's raining and those recent days when time went too slow and too fast all at once, I cried and smiled together. My tears acknowledged a life ended too young, the pain of the illness, the hurt of lost dreams and free spirits. With the smile I now could go on myself, in what we think of as reality, at last sure in the deepest part of my heart that I had counted after all.

THANK YOU, J.P. SOUSA
2007

I never heard him play
the glockenspiel
by the time my brother
could and did
I had left for college

Yet that dinging descant
in the "Washington Post March"
makes me think of him
clawing his elegant
way through high school
knowing in his guts
even as he paraded
with his glock at Sunday drills
that he'd have to ditch
those Junior ROTC khakis
to even knock on the door of real life

The summer before I left
he squeezed "The Sidewalks of New York"

from someone's abandoned accordion
and plunked tunes from *Kiss Me Kate*
and *Oklahoma!* on our tinny spinet
he'd even talked his way into fugues
and partitas with his keyboard
teacher, who had worked a deal
for practice time on a church pipe organ

Freshman year he'd found
he could exit Grunt Co. B
and escape half the drills
and all the push-ups
by the expedient of music
instead of carrying an M-1 rifle
he wrapped his lips around the cold
mouthpiece of a horn, but the fit was bad
and shortly full of spit
then he realized glockenspiel bars
are kin to piano keys
even better, the glock player
marches at the back of the band
where deficient spit and polish
might get by unnoticed

Yesterday when I heard "Washington Post"
on the radio, with blatting horns
and thumping bass drum
it was the ping of the glock
that really caught my ears
its crystal solo obbligato floating
pure against crass and blaring brass

Maybe, by auditioning for marching band
instead of bumbling the manual of arms
for the junior drill sergeant
my Bach and Bernstein-loving brother
made his statement instead
of just choosing the best of the worst

After all, there is only
one glock per band

BEING HAWAIIAN
2009

Some years ago, a Hawaiian lawyer friend and I were walking behind three state legislators on Honolulu's King Street as they headed from lunch back to the Capitol, engrossed in a conversation we couldn't help but overhear.

"See them?" said my friend, as they outpaced us. "That's why it's so hard to get stuff done in the legislature. The Japanese guy and the haole are trying to make a deal. The Hawaiian wants to build a relationship."

It's true. Being Hawaiian is almost entirely about personal relationships.

I'm Hawaiian. My dad was half Hawaiian, my mother Swedish from North Dakota. In 1940, they bought a house in Kailua, O'ahu, that's still in our family. During my childhood, relatives and friends dropped in anytime. The grownups sat around talking story, the men drinking and the women catching up on their mending.

I'm sure my mother wished heartily for prior planning. I know my father reveled in the drop-ins. Of course, he did it himself, in turn. He had friends wherever he went, lots of Hawaiians, and other people, too. He drank with them, sang with them, played poker with them, talked politics with them, even worked with them.

When I was eighteen, sometimes the two little haole boys who lived in the house across from ours would knock on our front screen door—my dad never closed the heavy wood door because it made him feel like nobody was home. When I answered, one of the little guys would ask, "Can Mr. Bowman come out and play?"

If my father, Moffett Bowman, had been a legislator, he would have walked down King Street trying to build personal relationships with guys who only wanted to make deals.

My dad had grown up in the early 1900s, when Hawai'i was a new U.S. Territory and it seemed advisable to many to abandon hallmarks of Hawaiian life. By the Forties and Fifties, "Hawaiian" was artifactual in our house—a bowl of *poi* usually on the sideboard, and a smattering of words like "pau" and "puka" in our common vocabulary.

Only decades later did I realize that simply by behaving as his natural self, my dad had conveyed to me the core of being Hawaiian. All his relationships with people and with the land and the sea were personal. I began to see layers of connections with other people, with the entire natural world, with our ancestors and the spirit world.

Blood is important, too, because it often binds us in an obvious way, or calls to us when we are far off, whether we are expatriates or foreign-born. Yet some who are truly Hawaiian are not so by blood, but have been embraced by the community not only because of heart and conduct but in addition by means of *hānai*, a Hawaiian form of adoption, or marriage, or work. The flip side is that blood alone does not automatically mandate cultural knowledge or Hawaiian values and behavior.

Even a century ago, about the time my dad was born in 1910, the question "What is 'being Hawaiian'?" would never have occurred to anyone. Hawaiians were still about half the Island population, and still knew who they were, although they could see their Islands changing before their eyes under American policies that had started just before the turn of the twentieth century with U.S. annexation.

But now the question does come up. Why?

For one thing, now Hawaiians are only about twenty percent of Hawai'i's population. And, after nearly two centuries of ever more complex intermarriage, most of us, like me, are mixed-blood. For another, we've been educated primarily as Americans, so we lack a lot of cultural knowledge that started to disappear rapidly in my father's generation. Third, many of us are physically disconnected from our homeland. If we live in Hawai'i, we are rushing around, trying to make ends meet, without time enough to even notice our natural world. If we are among the equal number (about 200,000) living in the mainland U.S. or elsewhere, we are disconnected geographically.

Some of us identify with another part of our blood—Chinese, Japanese, Portuguese, haole or numerous others. For some, the Hawaiian is minor. In my dad's day, one of his Hawaiian cousins who married a haole put on her baby's birth certificate "Caucasian." The dark side sometimes also comes out in other ways, as it does among many colonized native peoples, in poverty and domestic violence, in the despair of alcoholism and drug addiction, in disproportionate rates of criminal conviction and serious health problems.

Now, in 2009, "What is 'being Hawaiian'?" will have many answers. Mine is that I have spent most of my adult life using my career as a writer to learn about the depths of being Hawaiian and to discover what that means to me personally. My decades-long quest has been part of a larger social movement, the reclamation of Hawaiian culture.

Blood was my starting point. But to me, the most important element in being Hawaiian now is rediscovering knowledge. It leads to the Hawaiian core, that connection with people, with the 'āina—the whole natural world—and with the ancestors and the spirits.

For me, the last element is taking guidance from my name. For decades, I suffered the shame of having no Hawaiian name at birth. But when I was in my mid-fifties, I finally realized that the name a fellow student casually gave me in high school is actually who I am: *Keala-o-Ānuenue*, The Path of the The Rainbow.

Now these elements—blood, seeking cultural knowledge, connection, and name—comprise my core. I can tell, because now that I have found them, I am filled with a wordless song celebrating being home in a sea of peace.

Like other Hawaiians, I love to be with others. If one person is cooking, we cram into the kitchen so close we're bumping 'okole. If two people are speaking, a dozen will join them to sprawl on a *hikie'e* talking story. The air is filled with aloha.

If I am by myself, I'm still not alone. I'm with the aloha of the ancestors and the spirits, and the 'āina, the entire environment of land, sea and sky.

For years my daughter ribbed me for having "sky ecstasy" every morning when we took the dog for an early walk on Kailua Beach. At that fresh hour of the day, I was so overcome with the beauty of the sky and clouds that I would gasp with joy. Then one day she confessed that maybe she was having "sky ecstasy" too.

She'd started to catch being Hawaiian, just as I had caught it wordlessly from my father. She and I are starting to meld with the sun and the stars, the moon and the tides. We don't just observe, we are the palms, the shadows, the passing clouds. We are the song of the wind and the rain. Metaphorically we have become our names. I am Keala-o-Ānuenue, The Path of the Rainbow. She is Leiokanoe, Wreath of Mountain Mist.

The term "Hawaiian" did not originate until somebody besides Hawaiians showed up in our Islands. Our aboriginal people simply were *kanaka maoli*, or true people. Most aboriginal people call themselves some variation of "true people." It doesn't mean the one true people for the whole world. It means the true people of this particular homeland.

True people. To me, that is what it is to be Hawaiian—to be a true person of this homeland. A person who strives for a *pono*—perfectly balanced, morally correct—relationship with place. A person who seeks the knowledge and inspiration of ancestors and the guidance of the spirits of this place in caring for fellow humans and the homeland in a way that honors the lives of future generations. A person who accepts this *kuleana*—responsibility—and uses his or her talents in joyfully fulfilling it.

The blood, seeking of knowledge, relationships on many levels, and looking to my name all add up to one thing. *Aloha piha*. The blessing of complete aloha.

DOZENS OF COUSINS
2014

Dozens of cousins
No one's keeping score
Dozens of cousins
Every time I turn around
There's a dozen more

First one born in twenty-five
It started a stampede
Twenty-eight by sixty-three
Following the lead
Second generation starts
Before the first is done
Dozens more are born to us
Aren't we having fun?

Dozens of cousins
No one's keeping score
Dozens of cousins
Every time I turn around
There's a dozen more

Cousins always in my face
Cousins at my back
Cousins underneath my bed
Cousins in a stack
Cousins playing ʻukuleles
Cousins singing songs
Cousins surfing at the beach
I want to go along

Don't tell my mother
We climbed the mango tree
Don't tell about the kiss
When you sat by me
Don't tell your father
We swiped some cigarettes
Took a swig of bourbon
Underneath the steps

Dozens of cousins
No one's keeping score
Dozens of cousins
Every time I turn around
There's a dozen more

Dozens of cousins
Like sisters and brothers
If this one doesn't want to play
I just pick another
Dozens of cousins
How many would that be?

Enough to go around the world
Holding hands with me

Dozens of cousins
No one's keeping score
Dozens of cousins
Every time I turn around
There's a dozen more
There's a dozen more
There's a dozen more

ALOHA, ANUHEA
1997

Her name was Anuhea. The last time I saw her, she had given me something as important as life itself. But it took me forty years to accept it as my own.

In Hilo in May of 1995, I met Hawaiian kūpuna Aunty Abbie Napeahi and Uncle Howard Peʻa when I was researching an article on the spiritually based Hawaiian family counseling process hoʻoponopono. Aunty Abbie carefully explained the steps of hoʻoponopono, from finding the core problem to forgiving all parties involved and cutting loose from the pain. And then, part-way through the interview, she gently shifted the focus from hoʻoponopono to me.

Aunty Abbie asked me to lay before them the problem deepest in my heart, the one giving me the most pain in my life. In my mind I quickly reeled through classic candidates: Money. Marriage. Family. None of them seemed to warrant hoʻoponopono.

Then I did the bravest thing I've ever done. For the first time, I named out loud the gaping, lifelong hole in my heart: "Although I am Hawaiian by blood, I'm not sure I am a worthy Hawaiian."

I told them my Hawaiian school's mission had been to turn us into haole. My haole mother and Hawaiian father both had done the same.

My mind reeled off more reasons: I knew no more than a couple hundred isolated words of my language. I didn't even look very Hawaiian. My Hawaiian grandmother had died when my father was a baby, and no one ever passed down to us the knowledge of our guardian spirits, the ʻaumākua. Pain flooded me as if I had ripped a bandage from an open wound.

I did not voice my last, dark secret: I didn't have a proper Hawaiian name, one my family gave me. Without a Hawaiian name, I thought I had no lineage, no place with my ancestors, no heritage: I was nobody. The fact had burst forever into my consciousness when I first enrolled at Kamehameha Schools in the seventh grade. Unlike public school, where my class had only three Hawaiians, all four hundred girls at Kamehameha were Hawaiian. Almost all my classmates had both English and Hawaiian given names.

In tenth grade, in the fall of 1955, Anuhea Nahale-ā brought my problem to the surface. She and I, and about forty other sophomores, boarded in Dorm K at the top of the Kapālama Heights campus.

About four o'clock one rare afternoon when we were free from the dorm's scheduled after-school tasks like washing and ironing, Anuhea asked me to cut her hair. She'd asked me to do this several times before, though we weren't in the same academic section and didn't know each other very well.

That day she sat in my room with a towel clipped around her neck with a wooden spring clothespin. As I snipped at her unruly waves, she said, "Eh, what's your Hawaiian name?"

I could barely admit I didn't have one.

She said matter-of-factly, "I give you one." She didn't speak again until just before the haircut was over. "Keala-o-Ānuenue," she said. "The Path of the Rainbow."

The name was beautiful, in sound and in concept. I didn't dare ask why she chose it for me. I loved it. But in the back of my mind I thought I mustn't use it because my parents hadn't given it to me. "Keala-o-Ānuenue" felt *kapu* to me. I would be a thief to call myself The Path of the Rainbow. So I didn't use the name. But I couldn't forget it.

After we graduated, I went away to college in Minnesota, where people thought Hawai'i was a foreign country. Occasionally, one of the more worldly people asked me about my Hawaiian name. "Keala-o-Ānuenue. The Path of the Rainbow." And I explained that Anuhea had given it to me, aching in my heart because it wasn't a "real" name. The ache became bigger—an elusive, ghostly void. By the time I was thirty, sometimes I wept from the chronic pain, but still I did not know its source. I had moved to Oregon and was visiting Hawai'i more often—a mixed blessing, for in Hawai'i I was far more likely to meet someone who would ask the dreaded question that had become the symbol of my grieving heart. I could lie and say I didn't have a Hawaiian name. But

I wanted my name. Yet, each time I spoke it, I always added the disclaimer: I got the name at school.

I mentioned none of the name agony to Aunty Abbie and Uncle Howard. My doubtful worth as a Hawaiian was enough.

Now the room filled with Aunty Abbie's mana, her life force, her spiritual power. I felt like I was swimming safely in a deep ocean of no-nonsense love.

"You must stop blaming your parents and your school," she said, touching my arm and looking deep into my puka heart with her wise eyes. "Look at what they did give you. They gave you the power to write, the power to do your work. Let go of the blame. And never use it for an excuse again."

Instantly I felt myself do exactly as she said. I began to weep in relief. The time had come for the puka to heal.

Uncle Howard asked my Hawaiian name. "Keala-o-Ānuenue," I said, barely able to speak. "Oh, yes, The Path of the Rainbow," he replied, calmly accepting something I hadn't been able to accept for myself. Tears poured down my face. And then Uncle Howard and Aunty Abbie folded me up in their arms and their hearts and told me the name was a special gift—a gift of honor, a name I had grown into, for I had become a writer with the power to touch people's hearts, a writer who writes about Hawaiians, who are the heart of the rainbow.

And then they said, "Welcome home, Keala-o-Ānuenue."

In the weeks that followed, I came to understand that forty years earlier, on the day of the haircut, Anuhea had given me the answer to the question I had spent my life asking myself: Who am I? All I had to do was grow into the answer, bare my heart, accept the truth of the gift. Now I can speak the simple answer. I am Keala-o-Ānuenue.

I know now in my heart that our Hawaiian names are metaphors bundled in multiple meanings that we grow into. However we receive them, our names are a means by which we know we belong to our homeland, our ʻāina.

My name is Keala-o-Ānuenue, The Path of the Rainbow. I thank Anuhea for the name I have become.

NO NA PUA
1999

The day you wed
the time was high tide
when you stood on the beach
in ceremony.

You asked me to accept a lei
for Peter, my brother
for Dad, you said
Oh, and that's not all
you know where he is
will you please deliver it?

Ten, no eleven years now
he's been in the sea
where we lifted his ashes
from a pūʻolo at dawn
to spread them in swirling waters
to live where we had always lived

And so it was
at your wedding's end
I took your charge
your father's friend Lopaka
nodded at me, and I knew it was time
I handed him
my own lei from my neck
and took your lei
in a new pūʻolo in my hand
your bridal gift for Dad

Lopaka said, No, wait
another lei, from me
fragrant white ginger twined
with the green power of woven ti
this one from Lindsey
feather blaze of ʻohai aliʻi
he laid these, and my lei over my wrist
enveloped me in his arms
and we sobbed and sobbed

I know you could see our
great gasps of weeping
but did you hear us whisper ragged
"We loved him so much?"

And then we parted
I into the sea at your request
a slow march
to the high tide bursting.
I held na lei high on my arm

your pūʻolo up in my other hand
the water dimming green and gray
the last-light sky translucent blue
clouds gold-rimmed
in the waning sun of Kāne

I shouted to the sea
Mahalo no kēia lā
thank you for this day

At last I marched past break line
into the blue neck-deep
gave up my footing, swam free
turning landward, moving with the current
I saw you on the beach
you and John and *na pua*
All our children

I released my own lei
as on the day we strewed his ashes
I let loose the ʻohai aliʻi
then the ti
swells rose and fell, and I with them
you waited and watched
the sea throbbed
like the beat of our hearts
and pulse of our blood

I unwound your pūʻolo
unwound your lei within
the procession of *na lei*

danced west upon the current
west to the setting sun
west in the time of the long-shadowed day
when sometimes Peter and I—
were we eight and twelve
or just a little older?—
could not ignore the call
and we'd dash into the water
wearing all our clothes

Na lei danced west and still you stood
I surfed a fine swell
praying I wouldn't tumble
to the bottom
but knowing if I did
Peter would be laughing
as it was, this run
would have won a nickel bet
in those yesterdays so long ago

I caught the wave
and I was with him, your Dad
whose one wish
in the long weeks of the last summer
was just to go to the water
I was with him
and with the rest of them in the sea
and with all of you on the sand
na pua

And then in the windward twilight
I came from the waters
of Peter and family gone on
into your smiles
blotching you wet with salt
and knowing then our truths
Hawaiian hearts last forever
the sea is our refuge, our peace, our bond

So go to the sea, my dears
na pua, my children
all of you, go to the sea
to heal all wounds
to cure the heart
to share the soul
for the sea holds all
the past
the now
the yet to come

Go to the sea, my dears
and know to say
mahalo no keia lā
thank you for this day

TRUE GRATITUDE
1995

February, midsummer on Aitutaki. At 6:30 a.m. I sweat just from brushing my teeth. The atoll, nearly central in the fifteen Cook Islands strung through 770,000 square miles of ink-blue ocean, swelters in its turquoise lagoon twelve hundred miles south of the equator. On a map of the Pacific these specks of land might be a printing error.

This morning my daughter, Tamara, and I have hired a fisherman named Ma Tai to ferry us to Maina, a little-visited islet. Ma is gray-haired, lean and leather-brown, lacking one front tooth and the two middle fingers of his left hand.

Ma reminds me of an old family friend. My ancestors were native Hawaiian, and in addition to relaxation I have come here hoping to discover my roots in larger Polynesia. Some connections are obvious: the volcanic mountains of Rarotonga, the main island, look like a miniature of my home island of Oʻahu almost three thousand miles north. And as once was the case in Hawaiʻi, brown faces are everywhere—more than ninety percent of the population here are Cook Island Maori.

Maori means "the true people." In Hawaiian the same meaning belongs to the word *māoli*, but hardly anyone uses the term. The number of full-blooded Hawaiians, perhaps eight thousand, is now officially "statistically insignificant." Few people speak the native language, and fewer still have so much as a house-lot of ancestral land.

In the Cook Islands we hear Maori spoken as often as New Zealand-accented English. The Maori have their language, their blood, their land. Island real estate is all ancestral: People use it, but it cannot be bought or sold.

Ma searches for English words the way he sorts through his bait bucket for the right lure. He hands us each a three-hundred-yard spool of forty-pound-test nylon monofilament, hook and plastic squid on the end. We immediately strike two fish. Tamara hauls in her line in a neat pile; I build a sixty-foot snarl in the bottom of the boat. Ma just smiles, takes my tackle, and patiently rewinds.

Midmorning we disembark in Maina's sandbar shallows. "Barbecue," Ma says. Beyond the pale gold beach, between pandanus and palms, he balances a cast-iron griddle on a log and two coconuts. Wielding a French knife as a cleaver, he whacks each fish in thirds and flops the pieces on the grill with sliced breadfruit. Then he clutches the knife by the back of the huge, heavy blade and delicately peels a papaya.

"You eat. Please." Ma lays the food out on a rickety driftwood table. "Here. Plates." He hands us large, round leaves. Although I haven't felt hungry — it's still not much past 10:30 a.m.—with the first bite of fish I'm suddenly famished.

After snorkeling, we walk entirely around Maina, maybe half a mile, the texture of the sand underfoot and the coral patterns in the water changing every few steps. We pick up dozens of shells, every one occupied by a hermit crab. Ma sits in the shade of a pandanus checking over his fishlines and rolling stumpy cigarettes.

We head back in the mid-afternoon. The tide is so low that Ma cuts the motor and poles the last eighty yards. We step from the boat into bathtub-warm, foot-deep water. Salt mottles my thighs, and I can feel on my shoulders that my sunscreen didn't do much good.

"It's been a wonderful day, Ma," I say. "Thank you." I shake his five-fingered hand. His smile is as broad as his hat brim. He has spoken perhaps a dozen sentences all day. Now one more, seven words in eloquent order. "In my language," Ma says, "Thank you means *meitaki*."

ACKNOWLEDGMENTS

M ahalo nui loa to:

Ida May and Moffett Bowman, my letter-writing mother and my storyteller father, for setting me on the writing path very early by their examples and for encouraging me the rest of their lives.

My husband, David Walp, also a storyteller, for inspiring and encouraging me for nearly fifty years.

My brother, Pierre (Peter) Bowman, also a writer, whose work I admired and emulated.

My children and fellow writers, Tamara Leiokanoe Moan and Rolf Kaleohanohano Moan, whose critiques have boosted my work immensely.

The many teachers and editors who helped me grow as a writer.

All those who are crucial to these memoir pieces: My parents; my children; my aunties, especially

Nina and Betty; my twenty-eight Bowman cousins; Nora Chang and Mary Vincent; Nanette Chang Dettloff and Jackie Mahi Erickson; Vern Kimball and Freda McDonald; Argos the Border Collie, Betty Jenkins, Tom Moan, Cassy Bowman Rooney Monger, Ma Tai.

PUBLICATION NOTES

All the essays in *Huaka'i Hele* except "Being Hawaiian," "A Closing Conversation" and "Mother's Night" were published in *The Heart of Being Hawaiian* (Watermark, 2008). "Huaka'i" served as that book's introduction and has been slightly modified to appear here. The pieces listed below also appeared previously in the following magazines and literary journals:

"A Closing Conversation," *Northwest*, March 29, 1987

"Aloha, Anuhea," *Aloha*, November/December 1997

"Aloha, Ojibwa," *Honolulu*, March 1997 and *Gatherings*, a native peoples' anthology, Vol. VI, 1995

"Back to the Bastion," *Honolulu*, November 1999

"Being Hawaiian," *Hawai'i*, March/April 2009

"Father of Waters," *Honolulu*, December 1998

"Mother's Night," *Island Scene*, Spring 2004

"No Na Pua," *Ōʻiwi, A Native Hawaiian Journal*, 1999

"Princess Kaʻiulani and the Old Gray Mare," *Island Scene*, Winter 2004

"The Way Back," *Sierra*, September/October 1992

"True Gratitude," *Sierra*, January/February 1995

"Voice of the Beloved," *Honolulu*, August 2002 and *Sky Woman*, a native women writers' anthology, 2005

Student work excerpted in "Back to the Bastion" has been quoted with permission.

Sally-Jo Keala-o-Ānuenue Bowman grew up in Kailua, Oʻahu, born in 1940 to a half-Hawaiian father and a Swedish mother from North Dakota. She is a graduate of Kamehameha Schools and the Universities of Minnesota and Oregon. Her memoir pieces have appeared in various magazines and literary journals, and she is the author of *The Heart of Being Hawaiian* and co-author of *No Footprints in The Sand*, both published by Watermark Publishing of Honolulu. She lives in Springfield, Oregon, with her husband, David Walp.

www.ingramcontent.com/pod-product-compliance
Ingram Content Group UK Ltd.
Pitfield, Milton Keynes, MK11 3LW, UK
UKHW022006220326
11408UKWH00004B/494

9 781948 011457